Sad Songs
OF
Sorrow & Mourning
FOR THE
Ukulele

DICK SHERIDAN

To access audio, visit:
www.halleonard.com/mylibrary

Enter Code
1775-0012-7398-4014

ISBN 978-1-57424-392-5
SAN 683-8022

Cover by James Creative Group

Copyright © 2020 CENTERSTREAM Publishing
P.O. Box 17878 - Anaheim Hills, CA 92817

www.centerstream-usa.com | centerstrm@aol.com | 714-779-9390

Table of Contents

INTRODUCTION

And when I die don't bury me at all
Just pickle my bones in alcohol,
Put a bottle of booze at my head and feet
And then I know that I will keep

Dire deeds abound. Sorrowful accounts of tragedy and woe are abundantly represented in literature, theater, music, and art — as well as in today's real world. We seem to be surrounded by tales of murder, mayhem, and the micabre. Their history goes back to Cain and Abel, rollicks through the Middle Ages, and propels us up to the present in undiminished force. From poets and paintings, from Broadway and Hollywood, from radio, television, and the pages of daily newspaper, chilling examples are plentiful.

In music, songs of sadness, violence and foul play are no exception. They go back to ancient minstrelsy and run the gamut from grand opera to broadside ballads and cowboy laments of the Old West. There are songs depicting the tragic consequences of heartbreak, unfaithfulness, and unrequited love. Ballads recapture shoot-outs, robberies, train wrecks, sinkings, and a host of other disasters. And of course there's the enduring and predominant theme of murder.

Public broadcasting's Masterpiece is not opposed to a "wee bit of murder." Crime novelist Agatha Christie never fails to entice with such works as "Murder, She Wrote" and "Murder On The Orient Express." Among the dark deeds chronicled by Edgar Allen Poe there is "Murders in the Rue Morgue." Not to be forgotten is Shakespeare; he certainly has had his moments, like the ghost of Hamlet's father bewailing his demise as "murder most foul!" Dime store novelist Mickey Spillane offers his series of criminal dispatches and the not-to-be forgotten motto of "Live fast, die young, and have a good looking corpse!"

In popular currency we find country singer Johnny Cash singing about *The Long Black Veil* and from *Folsom Prison* *"I shot a man in Reno ..."* The Beatles jump in with *Maxwell's Silver Hammer.* Bluegrasser Ralph Stanley spares no punches with *O, Death,* heard in the soundtrack of the 2000 movie "Oh, Brother, Where Art Thou?" Munchkins from "The Wizard of Oz" gleefully celebrate with *Ding-Dong! The Witch Is Dead.* Bing Crosby and the Andrew Sisters beg for mercy in the 1943 chart topper with *Pistol Packin' Mama.* Bob Dylan has his *Knockin' On Heaven's Door* covered by rock group Guns N' Roses among others. Doc Watson offers *Little Sadie.* The Rodgers and Hammerstein musical "Oklahoma!" makes its contribution with *Pore Jud Is Daid.*

Our collection in this book encompasses reference to life's passing in all its many forms. Just as mortality is an unavoidable fact of life, it is just as unavoidable in song.

Some of the following songs of sadness commemorate historical events, factual or embroidered, while others draw from imagination. Romanticized versions of actual events appear like *The Wreck of Old 97* and the Titanic's sinking with "it was sad when the great ship went down ..." There are other melancholic songs of the sea and watery graves, along with poignant sentimental longings that are lovingly reflective, peaceful. Tender graveside laments are found in *Danny Boy* and the popular gaslight song from 1903, *Dear Old Girl.*

We'll encounter ghosts and gallows, and recall the children's chant of "Whenever you see a hearse go by ..." Two-timing lovers get their come uppance; a fallen knight lies beneath his shield. We'll remember a poor old slave who has gone to rest and another slave, revered and honored, interred in the trunk of an old hollow tree.

Although there is no dearth of death in song, not all is sinister, doom and gloom. There's comic relief and a touch of humor from barroom ditties and a boozy Irish wake. We'll have a good laugh beholding the Lord High Executioner or commiserating with a suicidal love-sick Dicky-bird (see Centerstream's "The Songs of Gilbert & Sullivan for Ukulele.") There's more too with *Clementine, Finnegan's Wake, Unfortunate Miss Bailey,* and the celebrated duel of *Abdullah Bulbul Amir.* And as an added aside consider this whimsical tombstone inscription:

> *Here lies the body of Elizabeth Bent*
> *Kicked up her heels and away she went*

It's important that we keep these songs in perspective. Remember many are works of imagination not to be taken literally. Some have stood the test of time for hundreds of years and have even become so-called "art songs." Certainly some will tug at your heart strings while others will prompt a reaction of "those rascals got what was coming to them." To ignore them is to ignore "the elephant in the room." They are here to stay, part of our culture and heritage, and ever more shall be so.

Two final references come by way of conclusion. One is from the headstone marking the grave of Scottish author and poet Robert Louis Stevenson (1850-1894) who was laid to rest on the Polynesian island of Samoa. The inscription is often titled "Requiem."

> *Under the bright and starry sky*
> *Dig my grave and let me lie:*
> *Glad did I live and gladly die*
> *And I laid me down with a will.*

This be the verse you 'grave for me:
Here he lies where he long's to be
Home is the sailor, home from the sea,
And the hunter home from the hill.

To this we add the uplifting opening and closing lines from John Donne's poem often called "Sonnet X". Donne was an English poet and cleric who lived from 1572 to 1631. The full poem was set for voice and piano by British composer Benjamin Brittain in 1945 after visiting the Nazi concentration camp Bergen-Belsen:

Death, be not proud,
though some have called thee mighty and dreadful,
for thou are not so ...
One short sleep past, we wake eternally
And death shall be no more;
Death thou shalt die.

ABDULLAH BULBUL AMIR

Ukulele tuning: gCEA

TRADITIONAL

For the numerous comical verses about the celebrated duel between Abdullah and the Russian Ivan Skavinsky Skivar, please refer to the Internet. Regretably there are too many to include here.

DANNY BOY

Ukulele tuning: gCEA

FRED E. WEATHERLY

DANNY BOY

DANNY BOY

THE BALLAD OF JESSE JAMES

Ukulele tuning: gCEA

TRADITIONAL

THE BALLAD OF JESSE JAMES

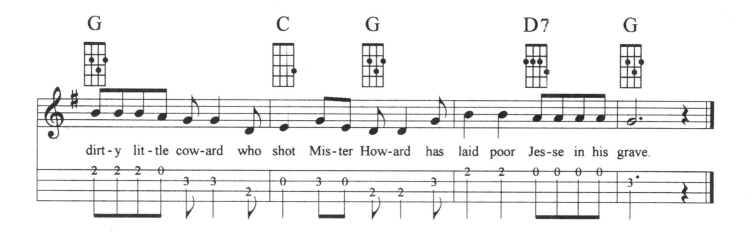

dirt-y lit-tle cow-ard who shot Mis-ter How-ard has laid poor Jes-se in his grave.

2. Jesse was a man,
A friend to the poor,
He'd never see a man suffer pain,
And with his brother Frank
He robbed a Chicago bank
And stopped the Glendale train.

3. It was on a Wednesday night,
The moon was shining bright,
They stopped the Glendale train,
And the people they did say,
For many miles away,
It was robbed by Frank and Jesse James.

4. Now the people held their breath
When they heard of Jesse's death
And wondered how he ever came to fall.
Robert Ford, it was a fact,
Shot Jesse in his back
When Jesse hung a picture on the wall.

Many additional lyrics and versons of this song exist, several of which can be found on the Internet. References in the song: Robert Ford who killed Jesse was a member of Jesse's gang. Mr. Howard was an alias Jesse was using at the time of his death when he was living in St. Joseph, Missouri.

BANKS OF THE O-HI-O

Ukulele tuning: gCEA

TRADITIONAL

2. Then only say that you'll be mine
And in no other arms entwine.
Down beside where the waters flow,
Down by the banks of the O-hi-o.

3. I held a knife against her breast,
As into my arms she pressed.
She said, "Oh, Willie, don't you murder me,
I'm not prepared for eternity."

4. I took her by her lilly white hand,
And dragged her down where the waters stand,
I picker her up and threw her in
And watched her as she floated down.

5. I wandered home twixt twelve and one,
Crying, "My God, what have I done!"
I murdered the only girl I ever loved
Because she would not be my bride.

BARBARA ALLEN

2. All in the merry month of May
The green buds they were swelling,
Sweet William on his death bed lay
For the love of Barbara Allen.

3. He sent his servant to her door,
To the place where she was dwelling,
"O Miss, O Miss, O come you quick,
If your name be Barbara Allen."

4. O slowly, slowly she got up,
And slowly she came nigh him,
She drew the curtains to one side
And said, "Young man, you're dying."

BARBARA ALLEN

5. "Yes, I am sick and very sick,
And grief is in me dwelling,
No better, no better I'll ever be
If I don't get Barbara Allen."

6. "Do you remember the other night
When you were at the tavern?
You drank a health to the ladies all
but you slighted Barbara Allen."

7. "Yes, I remember the other night
When I was at the tavern,
I drank a health to the ladies all
And my heart to Barbara Allen.

8. He turned his pale face to the wall,
For death was in him dwelling,
"Goodbye, goodbye, my dear friends all,
Be kind to Barbara Allen."

9. As she was walking toward her home,
She heard the death-bell knelling,
And every stroke it seemed to say,
"Cold-hearted Barbara Allen!"

10. She looked to the east, she looked to the west,
She saw the corpse a-coming,
"O hand me down that corpse of clay
That I may look upon it."

11. "O mother, mother, make my bed,
O make it long and narrow,
Sweet William died for me today,
I shall die for him tomorrow."

12. "O father, father, dig my grave,
O dig it long and narrow,
Sweet William died for love of me,
And I will die for sorrow."

13. A rose, a rose grew from William's grave
From Barbara's grew a briar,
They grew and they grew to the steeple-top
Till they could grown no higher.

14. They grew and they grew to the steeple-top
Till they could grow no higher,
And there tied in a true-love knot,
The rose clung round the briar.

THE BLUE TAIL FLY

Ukulele tuning: gCEA

TRADITIONAL

2. And when he'd ride in the afternoon,
I'd follow after with a hickory broom;
The pony being like to shy
When bitten by the Blue Tail Fly.
CHORUS

3. One day he ride around the farm,
The flies so numerous, they did swarm,
One chanced to bite him on the thigh,
The devil take the Blue Tail Fly.
CHORUS

4. The pony run, he jump, he pitch,
He threw my master in the ditch.
He died and the jury wondered why,
The verdict was the Blue Tail Fly.
CHORUS

5. They laid him under a 'simmon tree,
His epitath is there to see:
"Beneath this stone I'm forced to lie,
A victim of the Blue Tail Fly."
CHORUS

BURY ME BENEATH THE WILLOW

Ukulele tuning: gCEA

TRADITIONAL

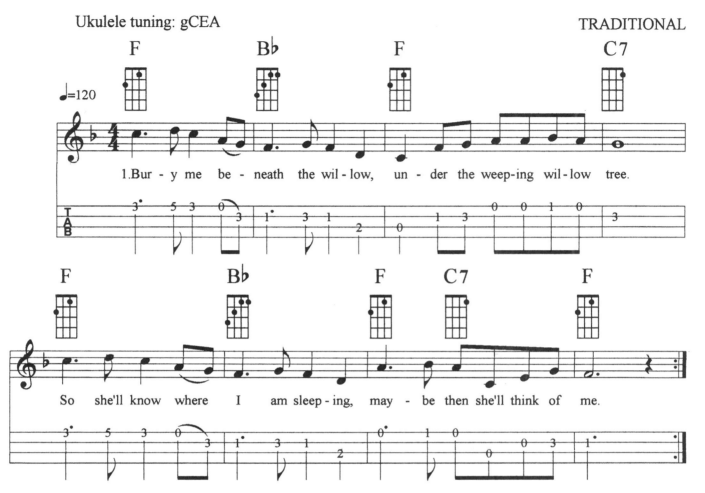

2. My heart is sad and I am lonely
For the only one I love,
When shall I see her, oh, no never,
'Till we meet in heaven above.

3. She told me that she dearly loved me,
How could I believe it untrue,
Until the angels softly whispered,
She will prove untrue to you.

4. Tomorow was to be our wedding,
Lord, oh Lord, where can she be?
She's out courting with another
And no longer cares for me.

5. Place on my grave a snow-white lily
To prove my love for her was true,
To show the world I died of grieving
For her love I could not win.

STAGOLEE

Ukulele tuning: gCEA

TRADITIONAL

2. Stagolee shot Billy de Lyons, what do you think about that?
   Shot him down in cold blood because he stole his Stetson hat.
   He was a bad man, that mean old Stagolee.

3. Billy de Lyons said, "Stagolee, please don't take my life.
   I've got two little babies and a darling, loving wife."
   You are a bad man, you mean old Stagolee.

4. The judge said, "Stagolee, what you doing in here?
   You shot Billy de Lyons, you gonna die in the 'lectric chair."
   He was a bad man, that mean old Stagolee.

5. Twelve o'clock they killed him, he held his head up high,
   Last thing Stagolee said was, "My six-shooter never lied."
   He was a bad man, that mean old Stagolee.

BURY ME NOT ON THE LONE PRAIRIE

Ukulele tuning: gCEA

TRADITIONAL

2. "Oh, bury me not," and his voice failed there,
But they took no heed of his dying prayer.
In a narrow grave, just six by three,
There buried him there on the lone prairie.

3. "Oh, bury me not on the lone prairie
Where the coyotes howl and the wind blows free,
Where there's not a soul who will care for me,
Oh, bury me not on the lone prairie."

Considered to be the most famous of cowboy
ballads, the song is based on a poem by E.H.
Chapin, – a dying sailor's lament entitled The
Ocean Burial whose words begin "O bury me
not in the deep blue sea ..." Variously entitled
The Cowboy's Lament, The Dying Cowboy and
Bury Me Out on The Lone Prairie, it is similar in
words and music to *Carry Me Back to the Lone
Prairie* made popular by Eddy Arnold, The
Sons of the Pioneers and many other country
performers.

THE BUTCHER BOY

Ukulele tuning: gCEA

TRADITIONAL

THE BUTCHER BOY

25

2. I wish, I wish, I wish in vain
I wish I was a maid again.
A maid again I n'er will be
Till cherries grow on an apple tree.

3. I wish my baby it was born
And smiling on his daddy's knee,
And my poor body to be dead and gone
With the long green grass growing over me.

4. She went upstairs to go to bed,
And calling to her mother said,
"Give me a chair till I sit down
And pen and ink will I write down."

5. At ev'ry word she dropped a tear,
And at ev'ry line cried, "Willie, dear,
Oh, what a foolish girl I was
To be led astray by a butcher boy."

6. Upstairs her father the door he broke
And found her hanging from a rope.
He took a knife and cut her down
And in her pockets there words he found:

7. Make my grave large, wide and deep,
 Put a marble stone at my head and feet,
And in the middle a turtle dove
So the world may know I died for love.

BALLAD OF CAPTAIN KIDD

Ukulele tuning: gCEA

TRADITIONAL

BALLAD OF CAPTAIN KIDD

2. My parents taught me well, as I sailed, as I sailed,
My parents taught me well, as I sailed,
My parents taught me well, to shun the gates of hell,
But against them I rebelled, as I sailed.

3. I'd a Bible in my hand, etc. (3 times)
By my father's great command,
But I sank it in the sand, as I sailed.

4. I murdered William Moore, etc. (3 times)
And I left him in his gore,
Not many leagues from shore, as I sailed.

5. I spied three ships from France, etc. (3 times)
And to them I did advance,
And sunk them all by chance, as I sailed.

6. I spied three ships of Spain, etc. (3 times)
I fired on them amain,
Till most of them were slain, as I sailed.

7. I'd ninety bars of gold, etc. (3 times)
And dollars manifold,
With riches uncontrolled, as I sailed.

8. Overtaken now at last, etc. (3 times)
And into prison cast,
My sentence being passed.

9. Farewell the raging main, I must die, I must die,
Farewell the raging main, I must die,
Farewell the ragin main, and Turkey, France and Spain,
I shall never see again, I must die.

Captain William Kidd, a Scottish seafarer, is probably history's most infamous pirate. Surrounded by legends of swashbuckling adventure, buried treasure, and treachery on the high seas, he was tried for his crimes by the British Admiralty, convicted, and twice hanged -- the first time the rope broke. His body was gibbited over the River Thames as a warning for those inclined to piracy.

COCKLES AND MUSSELS

Ukulele tuning: gCEA

TRADITIONAL

COCKLES AND MUSSELS

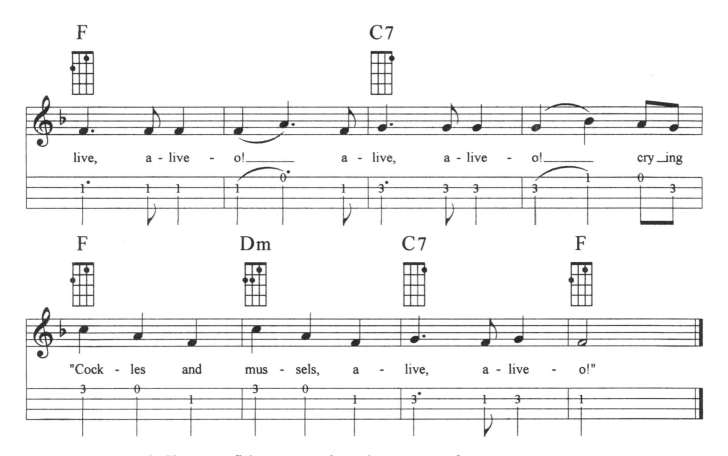

2. She was a fishmonger and sure 'twas no wonder,
Her father and mother were fishmongers too,
They wheeled their wheelbarrows through streets wide and narrow,
Crying, "Cockles and mussels, alive, alive-o!"
CHORUS

3. She died of a fever and no one could save her,
And that was the end of sweet Molly Mallone.
Now a ghost wheels her barrow through streets wide and narrow,
Crying, "Cockles and mussels, alive, alive-o!"
CHORUS

DARLIN' COREY

Ukulele tuning: gCEA

TRADITIONAL

1.Wake up, wake up, Dar - lin' Cor - ey!___ What
makes you sleep so sound? Rev - e - nue of - fi - cer, he's a -
com - in'___ gon - na tear your still___ house down.

DARLIN' COREY

2. The last time I seen Darlin' Corey
She was sitting on the banks by the sea.
Had a pistol tied around her body,
And a banjo strapped on her knee.

3. Go 'way, go away, Darlin' Corey,
Quit hanging around my bed.
Cheap liquor's ruining my body,
Pretty women has gone to my head.

4. Go dig me a hole in the meadow,
Dig a hole in the cold, cold ground,
Dig a hole, a hole in the meadow,
Gonna lay Darlin' Corey down.

5. Can't you hear those bluebirds a-singing,
Can't you hear their mournful sound?
They're a-preachin' Corey's funeral
In some lonesome graveyard ground.

Another song that often provides extra lyrics for "Darlin' Corey" is "Little Maggie."
Here are several examples:

Yonder stands Little Maggie,
A dram glass in her hand,
She's a-drinkin' away her troubles
Fooling 'round with some other man.

The first time I seen Little Maggie
She was standing in the open cabin door.
Shoes and stockings in her hand,
Bare feet on the old wooden floor.

Pretty flowers were made for blooming,
Pretty stars were made to shine,
Pretty girls were made for loving,
Lttle Maggie was made for mine.

DOWN IN THE WILLOW GARDEN

Ukulele tuning: gCEA

TRADITIONAL

DOWN IN THE WILLOW GARDEN

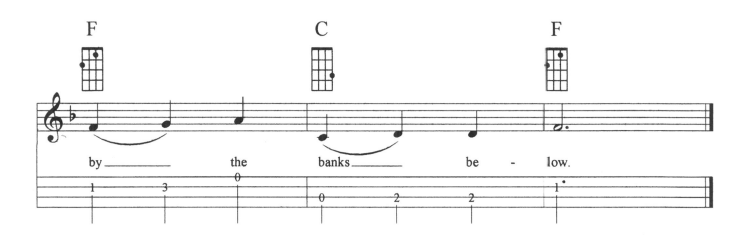

2. I drew my sabre through her,
It was a bloody night;
I threw her in the river,
Which was a dreadful sight.
My father often told me
That money would set me free
If I would murder that poor lttle girl
Whose name was Rose Connelly.

3. He stands now at his cabin door
Wiping the tears from his eyes,
For his only son soon shall walk
To yonder scaffold high.
My race is run, beneath the sun,
The scaffold now waits for me,
For I did murder that poor little girl
Whose name was Rose Connelly.

Sections of this melody reflect the Irish drinking song "Old Rosin The Beau." The tune is no stranger to the folk music process and has been used for political campaigns, slave songs, and even comic variations like "Acres Of Clams." The traditional lyrics tell of a person nearing life's end :

I traveled this wide world over
And now to another I'll go,
I know that good quarters are waiting
To welcome Old Rosin the Beau.

THE DREADFUL WIND AND RAIN

Ukulele tuning: gCEA

TRADITIONAL

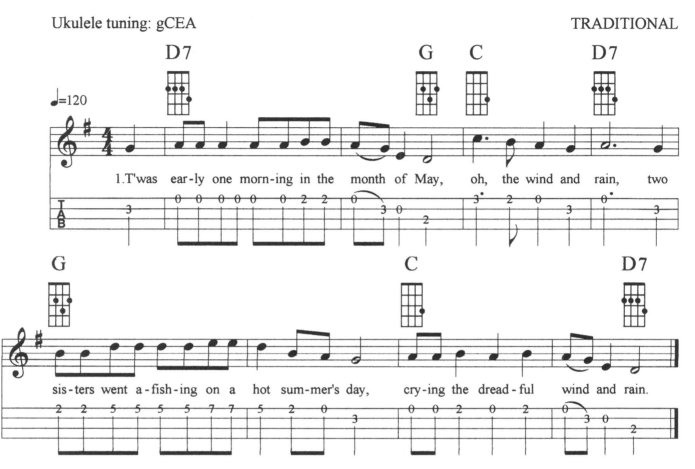

Note: This song is unusual since it starts and ends on the dominant D7th chord

2. Two sweet sisters, side by side,
Oh, the wind and rain,
Each one wishing to be Johnny's bride,
Oh, the dreadful wind and rain.

3. Johnny gave the young one a golden ring, etc.
But to the older one nary a thing, etc.

4. The sisters went a-walking by the water's brim, etc.
The older one shoved the younger one in, etc.

5. She shoved her in the river to drown, etc.
And watched her as she floated down, etc.

6. She floated down to the miller's pond, etc.
"Father, father, there swims a swan!" etc.

7. The miller fished her out with a pole and hook, etc.
And pulled that poor girl from the brook, etc.

35

8. He laid her on the bank to dry, etc.
A fiddler man came passing by, etc.

9. He saw that poor girl lying there, etc.
He took thirty strands of her long yellow hair, etc.

10. He made a bow of her long yellow strands, etc.
And fiddle pegs from the bones of her hand, etc.

11. He made a fiddle of her little breast bone, etc.
With a voice so sweet and a beautiful tone, etc..

12. And the only tune that fiddle could play,
Oh, the wind and rain,
The only tune that fiddle could play was
Oh, the dreadful wind and rain.

THE DYING BRITISH SOLDIER

Ukulele tuning: gCEA

TRADITIONAL

2. It was on December, the eighteenth day,
That our fleet set sail for Amerikay;
Our drums and trumpets loud did sound,
And then for Boston we were bound.

THE DYING BRITISH SOLDIER

3. And when to Boston we did come,
We thought the noise of the British drum
Would drive the rebels from that place
And fill their hearts with sore disgrace.

4. They said it was a garden place
And that our armies could with ease
Tear down their walls, lay waste their lands,
In spte of all their boasted bands.

5. We found a garden place, indeed,
But in it grew many a bitter weed,
Which soon cut off our highest hopes
And slowly wound the British troops.

6. For to our sad and sore surprise
We saw men like grasshoppers rise.
"Freedom or death!" was all their cry;
Believe they did not fear to die.

7. We sailed for York, as you've been told,
With the loss of many a Briton bold,
Full fifteen thousand have been slain,
Bold British heroes on the plain.

8. When I received my deathly wound,
I bid farewell to English ground.
My wife and children will mourn for me,
Whilst I lie cold in Amerikee.

EGGS AND MARROWBONE

Ukulele tuning: gCEA

TRADITIONAL

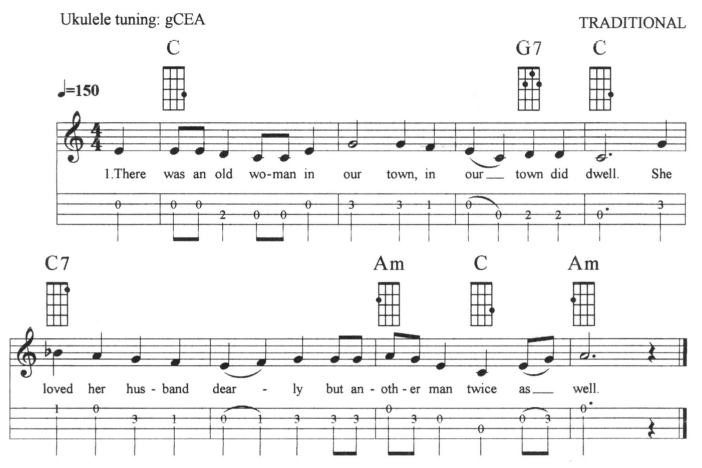

1.There was an old wo-man in our town, in our town did dwell. She
loved her hus-band dear - ly but an-oth-er man twice as well.

2. She went to see the doctor
To see what she could find.
To see what she could find, sir,
To make her old man blind.

3. Eggs, eggs, and marrowbone,
Feed them to him all,
That will make him so very blind
That he can't see you at all.

4. She fed him eggs and marrowbone,
Fed them to him all,
That did make him so very blind
That he couldn't see her at all.

5. Now that I am old and blind
And tired of my life,
I will go and drown myself
And that will end my strife.

EGGS AND MARROWBONE

6. To drown yourself, to drown yourself,
Now that would be a sin,
So I'll go down to the water's edge
And kindly push you in.

7. The old woman took a running jump
For to push the old man in,
The old man he stepped to one side
And the old woman she fell in.

8. She called for help, she screamed for help,
So loudly did she bawl.
The old man said, "I'm so very blind
That I can't see you at all."

9. She swam along, along swam she,
Till she came to the river's edge,
But the old man grabbed a big long pole
And pushed her further in.

10. Now the old woman is dead and gone
And the Devil's got her soul.
Wasn't she a foolish
Not to grab the old man's pole?

11. Eggs, eggs, and marrowbone,
Won't make your old man blind,
If you really want to do him in,
Just creep up from behind.

FINNEGAN'S WAKE

Ukulele tuning: gCEA

TRADITIONAL

FINNEGAN'S WAKE

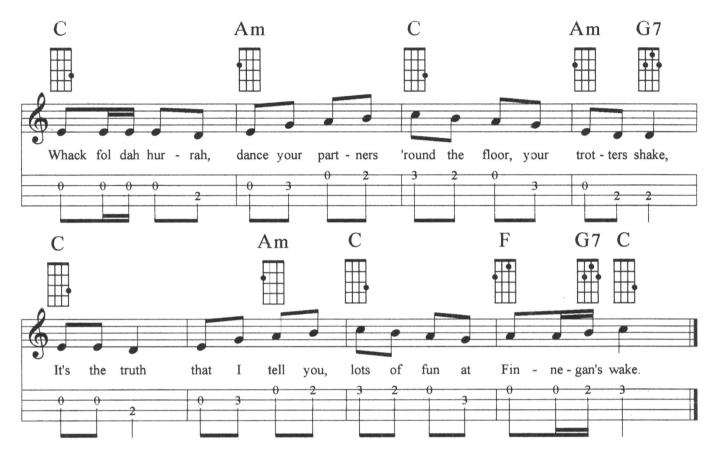

2. One morning Tim was rather full, his head was heavy which made him shake,
He fell off the ladder and broke his skull, so they carried him home a corpse to wake.

3. They wrapped him up in a nice clean sheet and laid him out upon the bed
With plenty of candles around his feet and a couple of dozen around his head.

4. His friends assembled at the wake, and Missus Finnegan called for lunch;
First they laid out tea and cakes, then pipes and tobacco and whiskey punch.

5. Then Biddy O'Brien began to cry, "Such a lovely corpse did you ever see?
Arrah! Tim avourneen, why did you die?" "Ah! none of your gab," said Biddy Magee.

6. Then Peggy O'Connor took up the job. "Arrah! Biddy," says she, "you're wrong I'm sure."
But Biddy gave her a belt on the gob and left her sprawling on the floor.

7. Each side in war did soon engage, 'twas woman to woman and man to man,
Shillelagh war was all the rage, and a row and a ruction soon began.

8. Mickey Maloney raised his head when a gallon of whiskey flew at him,
It missed and landed on the bed. The whiskey scattered over Tim.

9. Bedad, he revives! See how he rises. Tim Finnegan jumping from the bed,
Crying while he ran around like blazes, "Thundering blazes, you think I'm dead!"

FRANKIE AND JOHNNY

Ukulele tuning: gCEA

TRADITIONAL

2. Frankie and Johnny went walking,
   Johnny in his brand new suit,
   "Oh, good Lord!" says Frankie,
   "Don't my Johnny look real cute."
   He was her man, but he was doin' her wrong.

3. Johnny says, "I've got to leave you,
   But I won't be gone very long.
   Don't wait up for me, Frankie,
   Or worry while I'm gone."
   He was her man, but he was doin' her wrong.

FRANKIE AND JOHNNY

3. Frankie went down to the pool hall,
   To buy herself a bottle of beer,
   She says to the fat bartender,
   "Has my Johnny-man been here?"
   He was her man, but he was doin' her wrong.

4. The bartender looks at Frankie,
   Looks her right in the eye,
   "Ain't gonna tell you no story,
   Ain't gonna tell you no lie,
   If he's your man, he's a-doin' you wrong."

5. "Ain't gonna tell you no story,
   Ain't gonna tell you no lie,
   I saw your Johnny 'bout an hour ago
   With a gal named Nellie Bly.
   If he's your man, he's a-doin' you wrong."

6. Frankie goes down to South 12th Street,
   Looks up in the window so high,
   And there she sees her Johnny
   A-kissin' that Nellie Bly,
   He was her man, but he was doin' her wrong.

7. Frankie pulls back her kimono,
   Pulls out an old Forty-Four,
   Rooty-toot-toot, that gal did shoot,
   And Johnny rolled over the floor,
   He was her man, but he was doin' her wrong.

8. There six men goin' to the graveyard,
   Six in an old-time hack,
   Six men goin' to the graveyard,
   But only five are comin' back,
   He was her man, but he was doin' her wrong.

9. This story ain't got no moral,
   This story ain't got no end,
   This story just goes to show you
   That there ain't no good in men,
   They'll do you wrong, just as sure as your born.

THE GALLOWS TREE

Ukulele tuning: gCEA

TRADITIONAL

Slack your rope, hangs a man, oh, slack it for a while, .I

think I see my fath - er com-ing, rid - ing man-y a mile. Oh,

Fath-er have you brought me gold, or have you paid my fee, or

have you come to see me hang-ing on the gal-lows tree? I

THE GALLOWS TREE

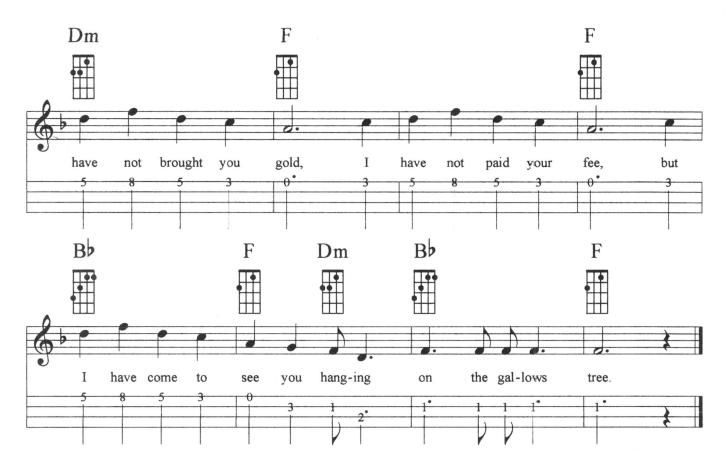

2. Oh, Mother have you brought me gold,
Or have you paid my fee?
I have not brought you gold, etc

3. Oh, Sister have you brought me gold,
Or have you paid my fee?
I have not brought you gold, etc.

4. Oh, Brother have you brought me gold,
Or have you paid my fee?
I have not brought you gold, etc.

5. Oh, Sweetheart have you brought me gold,
Or have you paid my fee?
I have brought you gold,
I have paid your fee,
Thank, God, my love you'll never hang
Beneath this gallows tree.

Other versions of this song deny the condemned man gold and a paid fee
leaving him to his sad fate.

GOLDEN VANITY

Ukulele tuning: gCEA

Traditional

2. Then up spoke our cabin boy, and bodly outspoke he,
  And he said to the captain, "What will you give to me,
  If I swim alonside of the Spanish enemy
  And sink her in the Lowland, Lowland, Low,
  And sink her in the Lowland sea?"

GOLDEN VANITY

3. "Oh, I will give you silver, and I will give you gold,
   And my own fair daughter your bonny brideshall be,
   If you'll swim alongside of the Spanish enemy
   And sink her in the Lowland, Lowland, Low,
   And sink her in the Lowland sea."

4. Then the boy he made him ready, and overboard sprang he,
   And he swam alongside of the Spanish enemy,
   And with his brace and auger in her side he bored holes three,
   And he sank her in the Lowland, Lowland, Low,
   And he sank her in the Lowland sea.

5. Then quickly he swam back to the cheering of the crew,
   But the captain would not heed him, for his promise he did rue,
   And he scorned his poor entreatings when loudly he did sue,
   And left him in the Lowland, Lowland, Low,
   And left him in the Lowland sea.

6. Then roundabout he turned, and he swam to the port side,
   And up unto his messmates full bitterly he cried,
   "Oh, messmates, draw me up for I'm drifting with the tide,
   And I'm sinking in the Lowland, Lowland, Low,
   And I'm sinking in the Lowland sea."

7. Then his messmates drew him up, but on the deck he died,
   And they stitched him in his hammock, which was so fair and wide,
   And they lowered him overboard, and he drifted with the tide,
   And he sank in the Lowland, Lowland, Low,
   And he sank in the Lowland sea.

GO TELL AUNT RHODY

Ukulele tuning: gCEA

TRADITIONAL

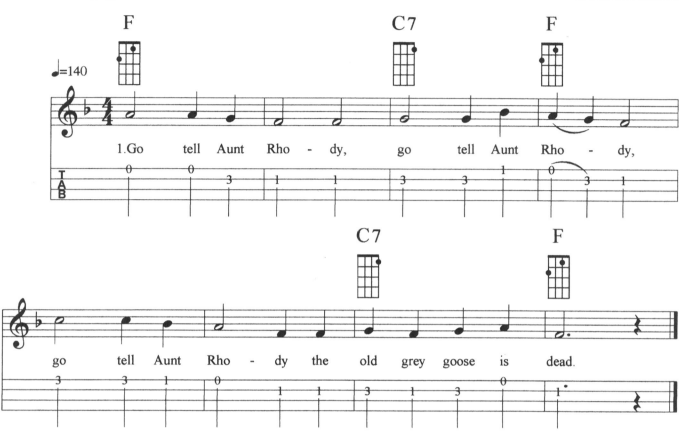

1.Go tell Aunt Rho - dy, go tell Aunt Rho - dy,

go tell Aunt Rho - dy the old grey goose is dead.

2. The one that she'd been saving, (3 times)
To make a feather bed.

3. The goslings are crying, (3 times)
Because their mammy's dead.

4. Died in the mill pond, (3 times)
Standing on its head.

THE GREAT SHIP TITANIC

Ukulele tuning: gCEA

TRADITIONAL

THE GREAT SHIP TITANIC

Four days into her maiden voyage from Southampton to New York, the RMS Titanic struck an iceberg and sank off the coast of Newfoundland on the morning of April 15, 1912. More than 1500 people lost their lives in what is considered the worst peacetime maritime disaster.

2. Oh, they built the ship Titanic to sail the ocean blue,
They thought it was a ship that water would never get through.
It was on its maiden trip that an iceberg hit the ship,
It was sad when the great ship went down.
CHORUS

3. Oh, they threw the lifeboats over in the dark and icy sea,
And the band began to play "Nearer My God To Thee."
Little children wept and cried as the waves swept over the side,
It was sad when the great ship went down.
CHORUS

4. They were in the North Atlantic, and they weren't far from shore.
The upper decks were for the rich, the lower for the poor,
It was on those decks below where the poor were the first to go,
It was sad when the great ship went down.
CHORUS

HAUL AWAY, JOE

Ukulele tuning: gCEA

TRADITIONAL

2. Louie was the King of France afore the revolution,
Way, haul away, we'll haul away, Joe.
But then he got his head cut off which spoiled his constitution,
Way, haul away, we'll haul away, Joe.

3. Once I had a German girl and she was fat and lazy, etc.
Now I've got a yeller girl, she darn near drives me crazy, etc.

4. St. Patrick was a gentleman, he come from decent people, etc.
He built a church in Dublin town, and on it put a steeple, etc.

5. Once I was in Ireland a-diggin' turf and praties, etc.
Now I'm on a lime-juice ship hauling on the braces, etc.

"Haul Away, Joe" is one of a class of sea songs known as Slow-Drag chanteys. These songs typically are short, simple, and were applied to brief tasks of hauling. The pull on the rope came when the word "Joe" was sung or shouted.

HENRY MARTIN

Ukulele tuning: gCEA

TRADITIONAL

♩=90

Dm

1. There were___ three broth-ers in mer-ry Scot-land, in mer-ry Scot-

Gm   **A**   **Dm**

land there were three,_____ and they did cast lots which of

Gm   **Dm**

them___ should go,___ should go,___ should go,___

F   **C**   **Dm**

for to turn rob-ber all on the salt sea.___

HENRY MARTIN

2. The lot it fell on Henry Martin,
The youngest of all of the three,
That he should turn robber all on the salt sea,
The salt sea, the salt sea,
For to maintain his two brothers and he.

3. He had not been sailing but a long winter's night,
Part of a short winter's day,
When he espied a stout lofty ship,
Lofty ship, lofty ship,
Coming and bearing on down him straight way.

4. "Hello, hello," cried Henry Martin,
"What makes you sail so nigh?"
"I'm a rich merchant ship bound for fair London Town,
London Town, London Town,
Will you please for to let me pass by?"

5. "Oh no, oh no," cried Henry Martin,
"That thing it never can be,
For I have turned robber all on the salt sea,
The salt sea, the salt, sea,
For to maintain my two brothers and me."

6. "Then lower your topsail and brail down your mizzen,
Bow youselves under my lee,
Or I shall give you a fast-flowing ball,
Flowing ball, flowing ball,
And send your dear bodies down in the salt sea."

7. Then broadside to broadside and at it they went,
For fully two hours or three,
Till Henry Martin gave to her the death shot,
The death shot, the death shot,
Heavily listing to starboard went she.

8. Bad news, bad news, to old England came,
Bad news to old London Town,
There's been a rich vessel, and she's cast away,
Cast away, cast away,
And all of her merry men drowned.

HIGH BARBARY

Ukulele tuning: gCEA

TRADITIONAL

HIGH BARBARY

2. "Now are you a pirate or a man-o'-war?" cried she,
Blow high, blow low, and so sailed we.
"We are not a pirate but a man-o'war!" cried we,
A-sailing down along the coast of High Barbary.

3. "Lower down your topsail and bring your vessel to, etc.
For we've got some letters to be sent home by you."

4. "We'll lower down our topsail and bring our vessel to, etc.
But only in a harbor and alongside of you." etc.

5. For broadside, for broadside, we fought on the main, etc.
Until the lofty frigate shot the pirate's mast away. etc.

6. With cutlass and gun we fought for hours, three, etc,
The ship it was their coffin and their grave it was the sea. etc.

7. "For quarter, for quarter!" the lusty pirate cried, etc.
But the quarter that we gave them was to sink them in the tide. etc.

8. And oh it was a cruel sight and grieved us full score, etc.
To see them all a-drowning as they tried to swim ashore etc.

I RIDE AN OLD PAINT

Ukulele tuning: gCEA

TRADITIONAL

2. Old Bill Jones had two daughters and a song,
One went to Denver the other went wrong.
His wife she died in a poolroom fight,
And now he keeps singing from morning to night.
CHORUS

3. Oh, when I die, take my saddle from the wall,
Put it on my pony, lead him out of his stall,
Tie my bones to his back, turn our faces to the west,
And we'll ride the prairies that we love the best.
CHORUS

✠

"I'm goin' to Montan' for the throw the
hoolihan." Hoolihan is a term for bulldogging,
which became an established rodeo sport
after 1900. Similar Sounding is hooley-ann, a
roping term of the cowboys used to describe a
quick throw with a small hoop. Popularized
by balladeer Margaret Larkin and playwright
Lynn Riggs. In 1931 Margaret Larkin published
the first book of cowboy songs that included
musical notation for all the selections.

JOHN BROWN'S BODY

Ukulele tuning: gCEA

TRADITIONAL

John Brown was a Northern abolitionist who advocated violent oppostion to slavery.
In 1859 he led a raid on the Federal armory at Harpers Ferry, West Virginia, in a failed
attempt to gain weapons for a slave rebellion. Brown was captured, tried for treason,
and executed. The raid is considered to have been a major factor in the start of the
Civil War. The song was popular with marching Union troops.

JOHN BROWN'S BODY

2. He captured Harpers Ferry with his nineteen men so true,
   He frightened old Virginia 'til she trembled through and through.
   They hanged him for a traitor, themselves the traitor's crew,
   His soul goes marching on. CHORUS

3. He's gone to be a soldier in the army of the Lord (3 times),
   His soul goes marching on. CHORUS

4. The stars above in heaven are a-lookin' kindly down (3 times),
   His soul goes marching on. CHORUS

5. We'll hang Jeff Davis from a sour apple tree (3 times),
   As we go marching on. CHORUS

JUG OF PUNCH

Ukulele tuning: gCEA

TRADITIONAL

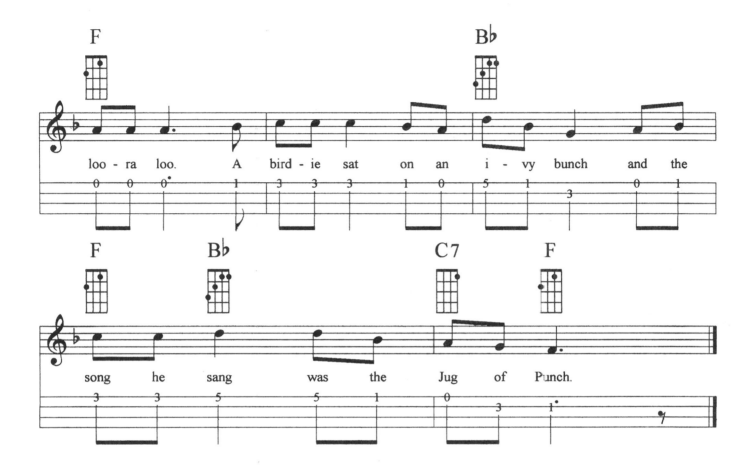

loo - ra loo. A bird - ie sat on an i - vy bunch and the

song he sang was the Jug of Punch.

2. What more diversion could a man desire
Then to sit him down by the ale house fire,
With a fine red pippin to crack and crunch
And on the table a jug of punch.
    Too-ra loo ... etc.

3. Let the doctor come with all his art,
He'll make no impression upon my heart.
Even the cripple forgets his hunch
When he's snug outside of a jug of punch.
    Too-ra loo ... etc.

4. And when I'm dead and in my grave,
No costly tombstone will I crave.
Just lay me down in my native peat
With a jug of punch at my head and feet.
    Too-ra loo ... etc.

THE KNOXVILLE GIRL

Ukulele tuning: gCEA

TRADITIONAL

1.I met a lit - tle girl in Knox - ville, a

town we all know well._____ And

ev - 'ry Sun - day eve - ning out

in her home I'd dwell._____ We

THE KNOXVILLE GIRL

2. She fell down on her bended knees,
For mercy she did cry.
"Oh, Willie dear, don't kill me here,
I'm not prepared to die."
She never spoke another word,
I only beat her more.
Until the ground around me
With her sweet blood did flow.

3. I took her by her golden curls
And dragged her round and round.
I threw her in the river
That flows through Knoxville town.
Go down, go down, you Knoxville girl,
With the dark and roving eye,
Go there, go there, you Knoxville girl,
You can never be my bride.

4. The police came down from Knoxville,
They placed me in a jail.
My friends could not a pardon get
Nor could they go my bail.
I'm here to waste my life away
Down in this dirty cell,
Because I killed that Knoxville girl,
The girl I loved so well.

"The Knoxville Girl" is derived from an Irish ballad of the 19th century, "The Wexford Ballad," which itself stems from an ealier English ballad "The Oxford Girl." The theme of a watery grave is common to many traditional songs including several in this book -- "Down in the Willow Garden," "Omie Wise," "The Dreadful Wind and Rain," " Banks of the O-Hi-O," and "Eggs and Marrowbone."

PRETTY POLLY

Ukulele tuning: gCEA

TRADITIONAL

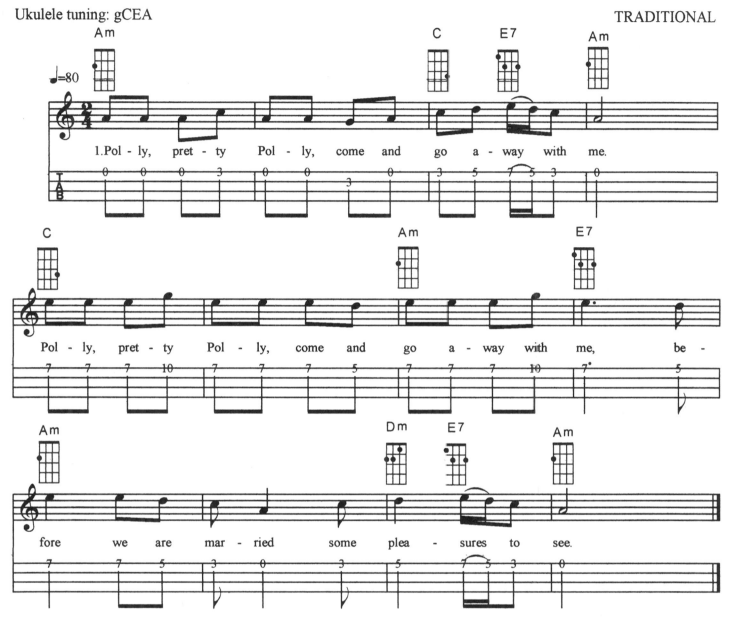

2. He courted pretty Polly all of the live long night, (2 times)
Then left her next morning before it was light.

3. She climbed the horse behind him and away they did go, (2 times)
Over hills and mounains and the valley below.

4. "Willie, oh Willie, I'm afraid of your ways, (2 times)
Afraid you will lead my poor body astray."

5. He stabbed her in the heart and the blood it did flow, (2 times)
And down into the grave poor Polly did go.

6. A debt to the devil Willie now must pay, (2 times)
For killing pretty Polly and for running away.

LILY OF THE WEST

Ukulele tuning: gCEA

TRADITIONAL

1.I just came down from Lou-is-ville some pleas-ure for to find;____ A hand-some girl from Mich-i-gan, so pleas-ing to my mind.____ Her ros-y cheeks, and roll-ing eyes like ar-rows pierced my breast,____ and they call her hand-some Mar-y, the Lil-y of the West.

LILY OF THE WEST

2. I courted her for many a day, her love I thought to gain;
Too soon, too soon she slighted me, which caused me grief and pain.
She robbed me of my liberty, deprived me of my rest,
They call her handsome Mary, the Lily of the West.

3. One evening as I rambled, down by yon shady grove,
I met a Lord of high degree, conversing with my love.
He sang, he sang so merrily, whilst I was sore oppressed,
He sang for handsome Mary, the Lily of the West.

4. I rushed up to my rival, a dagger in my hand,
I tore him from my true love, and boldly bade him stand;
Being mad to desperation, my dagger pierced his breast,
I was betrayed by Mary, the Lily of the West.

5. Now my trial has come on, and sentenced soon I'll be,
They put me in the criminal box, and there convicted me.
She so deceived the Jury, so modestly did dress,
She far outshone bright Venus, the Lily of the West.

6. Since then I've gained my liberty, I'll rove the country through,
I'll travel the city over, to find my loved one true.
Although she stole my liberty, and deprived me of my rest,
Still I love my Mary, the Lily of the West.

History of "Lily of the West" is rather cloudy. Some claim it as a traditional Irish ballad while others trace its roots to an English broadside street ballad. The currently popular version substitutes the name Flora for Mary. The song enjoys recordings by numerous artists including Joan Baez, Bob Dylan, the Irish group The Chieftains, and folk singers Peter, Paul & Mary. A number of variants can be found among them "The Lakes of Pontchartrain" and "The Buffalo Skinners"("The Hills of Mexico") whose lyrics begin:

> *It happened in Jacksboro, in the spring of seventy-three,*
> *A man by the name of Crego came stepping up to me,*
> *Saying, "How do you do, young fellow, and how would you like to go*
> *And spend one summer pleasantly on the range of the buffalo?"*

When it came time to settle up, Crego claimed the profits were all depleted by the drovers' drinking.

> *The season being near over, old Crego he did say,*
> *The crowd has been extravagent, was in debt to him that day.*
> *We coaxed him and we begged him, and still it was no go,*
> *We left old Crego's bones to bleach on the range of the buffalo.*

LITTLE SADIE

Ukulele tuning: gCEA

TRADITIONAL

1.Went out one night to make a lit-tle round, I met lit-tle Sa-die and I shot her down. I went back home and I got in bed, a four-ty four pis-tol un-der my head.

70

LITTLE SADIE

2. Woke up next morning 'bout a half-past nine,
The hacks and the buggies all standing in line,
Gents and the gamblers standing all round
Taking Little Sadie to her burying ground.

3. Then I began to think what I'd done,
I grabbed my hat and away I run,
Made a good run but a little too slow,
They overtook me in Jerico.

4. I was standing in the corner reading the bill
When up stepped the sherrif from Thomasville.
He said, "Young man, ain't your name Brown?
Remember the night you shot Sadie down?"

5. "I said, yes sir, my name is Lee,
I murdered Little Sadie in the first degree.
And the first degree and the second degree,
If you got my papers won't you read 'em to me."

6. They took me downtown and they dressed me in black,
Put me on the train and started me back.
They crammed me back in that Thomasville jail,
And I had no money for to go my bail.

7. The judge and the jury, they took their stand,
The judge had the papers in his right hand,
Forty-one days and forty-one nights,
Forty-one years to wear the ball and the stripes.

LORD RANDALL

Ukulele tuning: gCEA

TRADITIONAL

Bob Dylan used this question & answer form in his 1962
ballad "A Hard Rain's A-Gonna Fall." It starts out:
Oh, where have you been, my blue-eyed son?
Oh, where have you been, my darling young one?

LORD RANDALL

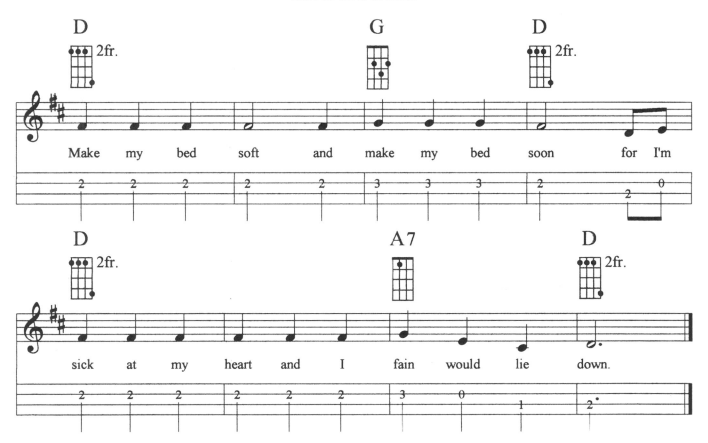

2. What did she give you, Lord Randall, my son?
What did she give you, my handsome one?
Fried eels in a pan, dear Mother,
Fried eels in a pan, dear Mother.
Make my bed soft and make my bed soon
For I'm sick at my heart and I fain would lie down.

3. I fear you are poisoned, Lord Randall, my son,
I fear you are poisoned, my handsome one.
Yes, I am poisoned, Mother,
Yes, I am poisoned, Mother,
Make my bed soft and make my bed soon
For I'm sick at my heart and I fain would lie down.

3. What are your leavings, Lord Randall, my son?
What are your leavings, my handsome one?
My hawks and my hounds, Mother,
My hawks and my hounds, Mother.
Make my bed soft and make my bed soon
For I'm sick at my heart and I fain would lie down.

4. And for your true love, Lord Randall, my son,
What will you leave to her, my handsome one?
A rope to hang her, Mother!
A rope to hang her, Mother!
Make my bed soft and make my bed soon
For I'm sick at my heart and I fain would lie down.

LORD THOMAS & FAIR ELLENDER

Ukulele tuning: gCEA

TRADITIONAL

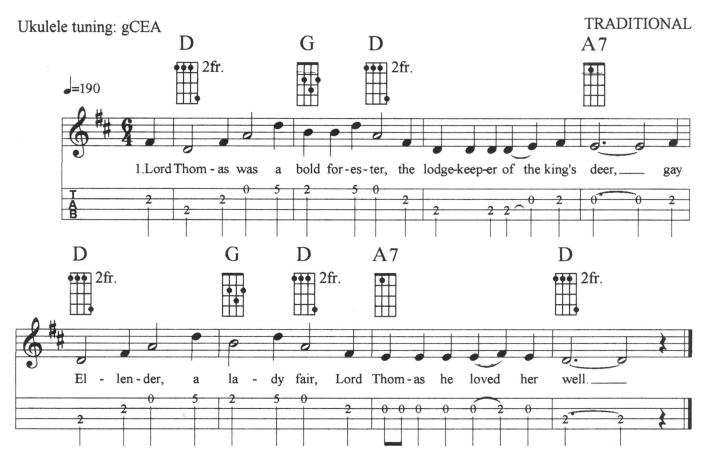

2. "Mother, dear Mother, come riddle to me,
Come riddle it all in one,
And tell me whether Fair Ellender to wed
Or bring the brown girl home.

3. "The brown girl she has house and land,
Fair Ellender she has none,
And there I charge you with the blessing
To bring the brown girl home."

4. He got on his horse and he rode and rode,
And he rode till he came to the home
Of one so ready as Fair Ellender herself,
To rise and bid him in.

5. "What news, what news, Lord Thomas," she said,
"What news have you brought unto me?"
"I've come to ask you to my wedding,
A sorrowful wedding to be.

6. "Bad news, bad news, Lord Thomas," she said,
Bad news you bring to me,
You've come to ask me to your wedding
When I your bride should be."

7. "Oh, Mother, oh, Mother, come riddle to me,
Come riddle it all in one,
If I must go to Lord Thomas' wedding
Or if I must stay at home?"

8. "Many may be your friends, daughter,
But thousands are your foe,
And therefore I charge you with my blessing,
To Lord Thomas' wedding don't go."

9. "Yes, many may be my friends, Mother,
And thousands are my foe,
But betide to my life, betide to my death,
To Lord Thomas' wedding I'll go."

10. She dressed herself in rich array,
Her sisters dressed in greeen,
And every town that they rode through
They took her to be some queen.

11. They rode and they rode 'till they came to the hall,
So loudly she twirled at the pin,
There was none as ready as Lord Thomas himself
To let Fair Ellender in.

75

12. He took her by her lily white hand
When leading her through the hall,
Saying, "Fifty gay ladies are here today
But here is the flower of all."

13. "Is this your bride," Lord Thomas, she said,
"She looks most wonderfully brown?
You might have had as fair a woman
As ever trod England's ground."

14. "Despise her not, Fair Ellender," he said,
"Despise her not to me,
Much better your little finger I like
Than I do her whole body."

15. The brown girl she was standng by
With knife ground keen and sharp,
Betwixt the long ribs and the short
She pierced Fair Ellender's heart.

16. "Oh, what is the matter? Lord Thomas he said,
"You look so pale and wan.
You used to have so fair a color
As ever the sun shone on."

17. "Oh, are you blind, Lord Thomas," she said,
Or can't you very well see,
And can't you see my own heart's blood
As it trickles down to my knee?"

18. Lord Thomas he was standing by
With sword ground keen and sharp,
Between the long ribs and the short
He pierced his own bride's heart.

19. He held the hilt against the wall,
The point against his breast,
Saying, "This is the ending of three true lovers,
God send our souls to rest."

20. "Oh, Mother, oh, Mother, go dig my grave,
Go dig it wide and deep,
And place Fair Ellender in my arms
And the brown girl at my feet."

MARY HAMILTON

Ukulele tuning: gCEA

TRADITIONAL

MARY HAMILTON

2. Word is to the kitchen gone, and word is to the hall,
And word is up to Madam Queen, and that is the worst of all,
That Mary Hamilton's born a child, to the highest Stuart of all.

3. "Arise, arise, Mary Hamilton, arise and tell to me
What hast that done with thy wee baby
I heard and I saw weep by thee?"

4. "I put him in a tiny boat and cast him out to sea,
That he might sink or he might swim
But he'd never come back to me."

5. "Arise, arise, Mary Hamilton, arise and come with me,
There is a wedding in Glasgow town,
This night we'll go and see."

6. She put not on her robes of black nor her robes of brown,
But she put on her robes of white
To ride into Glasgow town.

7. And as she rode into Glasgow town, the city for to see,
The baliff's wife and the provost's wife
Cried "Ach and alas for thee."

8. "You need not weep for me," she cried, "you need not weep for me,
For had I not slain my own wee babe,
This night I would not die."

9. "Last night I washed the Queen's feet and put the gold in her hair,
And the only reward I find for this
Is the gallows to be my share."

10. "Cast off, cast off my gown," she cried, "but let my pettcoat be,
And tie a napkin 'round my face,
The gallows I would not see."

11. Then by and by came the King himself, looked up with a pitiful eye,
"Come down, come down, Mary Hamilton,
Tonight you'll dine with me."

12. "Ah, hold your tongue, my soverign leige, and let your folly be,
For if you'd a mind to save my life
You'd never have shamed me."

*This Scottish ballad, sometimes called "The Four Marys" dates back to the 16th Century.
Mary Hamilton is an attendant to the Queen of Scots but has a child by the Queen's husband,
the King of Scots. Mary kills the infant and is sentenced to die for her crime.*

MATTY GROVES

Ukulele tuning: gCEA

TRADITIONAL

This song, known as a Border ballad, traces its ancestry back to the 17th century and comes from the north of England. It was collected by folklorist Francis James Child in his monumental work of 305 traditional songs from England, Scotland, and their American variants. The melody of which there are many versions is one often heard for the ballad "Shady Grove."

MATTY GROVES

And when the meeting it was done she cast her eyes about
And there she saw little Matty Groves walking in the crowd.

"Come home with me, little Matty Groves, come home with me tonight,
Come home with me, little Matty Groves, and stay with me tonight."

"Oh, I can't come home, I won't come home and stay with you tonight,
By the rings on your fingers I can see you are Lord Arnold's wife."

"'Tis true I am Lord Arnold's wife, Lord Arnold's not at home,
He is out to the far corn fields bringing the yearlings home."

A servant who was standing by, and hearing what was said,
He swore Lord Arnold he would know before the sun was set.

And in his haste to carry the news, he filled his breast and ran,
And when he came to the broad millstream he took off his shoes and swam.

Little Matty Groves he lay down and he took a little sleep,
When he awoke Lord Arrnold was standing at his feet.

Saying, "How do you like my feather bed, and how do you like my sheets,
But better still your lady gay who lies in your arms asleep?"

"Oh, well I like your feather bed, and well I like your sheets,
But better still your lady gay who lies in my arms asleep."

"Get up! Get up!' Lord Arnold cried, "get up as quick as you can,
It'll never be said in fair England that I slew a naked man."

"Oh, I won't get up, I won't get up, I can't get up for my life,
For you have two well beaten swords and I have but a pocket knife."

"It's true I have two beaten swords, they cost me deep in purse,
But you will have the better of them and I will have the worst."

"And you will strike the very first blow, and strike it like a man,
I will strike the very next blow and I'll kill you if I can."

So Matty struck the very first blow and he hurt Lord Arnold sore,
Lord Arnold struck the very next blow and Matty struck no more.

Lord Arnold then he took his wife, he sat her on his knee,
Saying, "Who do like the better of us, Matty Groves or me?"

Then up and spoke his own dear wife, never heard to speak so free,
"I'd rather kiss dead Matty's lips than you and your finery"

Lord Arnold he jumped up and loudly he did roar,
He struck his wife right through the heart and pinned her against the wall.

"A grave, a grave", Lord Arnold cried, "to put these lovers in,
But bury my lady at the top for she was of noble kin".

OH, MY DARLING, CLEMENTINE

Ukulele tuning: gCEA

TRADITIONAL

2. In a cavern, in a canyon,
Excavating for a mine,
Dwelt a miner, forty-niner,
And his daughter, Clementine.

3. Light she was and like a fairy,
And her shoes were number nine,
Herring boxes without topses
Sandals were for Clementine.

OH MY DARLING, CLEMENTINE

4. Drove she ducklings to the water
every morning just at nine,
Hit her foot against a splinter
Fell into the foaming brine.

5. Ruby lips above the water
Blowing bubbles soft and fine,
But alas, I was no swimmer,
Neither was my Clementine.

6. How I missed her! How I missed her!
How I missed my Clementine,
But I kissed her little sister
And forgot my Clementine.

OLD BLUE

Ukulele tuning: gCEA

TRADITIONAL

1.I had a dog ____ and his name was Blue, ____

____ and I bet-cha five dol-lars he's a good dog too. Say-ing, "Come on,

Blue, ____ you're a good dog, you." ____

2. Shouldered my axe, and I tooted my horn,
Gonna get me a possum in the new ground corn.
Saying, "Come on, Blue, I'm comin', too."

3. Chased that possum up a 'simmon tree,
Blue looked at the possum, possum looked at me.
Saying, "Go on Blue, you can have some too."

OLD BLUE

4. Baked that possum good and brown,
Laid them sweet taters 'round and 'round.
Saying, "Come on, Blue, you can have some too."

5. "Blue, what makes your eyes so red?"
"I've run them possom till I'm almost dead."
Saying, "Go on, Blue, I'm comin' too."

6. Old Blue died, and he died so hard,
He shook the ground in my backyard.
Saying, "Go on, Blue, I'm comin' too."

7. I dug his grave with a silver spade,
And I let him down with a golden chain.
Saying, "Go on, Blue, I'm comin' too."

8. When I get to heaven, first thing I'll do,
Grab my horn and I'll blow for Blue.
Saying, "Come one, Blue, finally got here too.

OMIE WISE

Ukulele tuning: gCEA

TRADITIONAL

2. He told her to meet him at Adams's Springs,
He promised her money and other fine things.

3. So fool-like she met him at Adams's Springs,
No money he brought her or other fine things.

4. "Go with me, little Omie, and away we will go,
We'll go and get married and no one will know."

5. She climbed up behind him and away they did go,
But off to the river where deep waters flow.

6. "John Lewis, John Lewis, will you tell me your mind,
Do you intend to marry me or leave me behind?"

7. "Little Omie, little Omie, I'll tell you my mind,
My mind is to drown you and leave you behind."

8. "Have mercy on my baby and spare me my life.
I'll go home as a beggar and never be your wife."

9. He kissed her and hugged her and turned her around,
Then pushed her in deep waters where he knew she would drown.

10. He got on his pony and away he did ride
As the screams of lttle Omie went down by his side.

11. 'Twas on a Thursday morning, the rain was pouring down,
When the people searched for Omie but she could not be found.

12. Two boys went a-fishing on a fine summer day
And saw little Omie's body go floating away.

13. They threw their net around her and drew her to the bank,
Her clothes were all wet and muddy, they laid her on a plank.

14. They sent for John Lewis to come to that place
And brought her out before him so he might see her face.

15. He made no confession but they carried him to jail,
No friends or relations would go on his bail.

The death in 1808 of Naomi Wise, an 18 year old orphan girl, was documented in song shortly after her pregnant and battered body was found floating in a river. Her n'er-do-well boy friend Johnathan Lewis was accused of the crime and was jailed. But before being brought to trial Lewis managed to escape. Later recaptured he was tried not for Omie's murder but for the prison break and received a prison sentence of only 47 days. Omie's body is interred in a Randolph County Cemetery in North Carolina close to the scene of the crime.

PETER GRAY

Ukulele tuning: gCEA

TRADITIONAL

PETER GRAY

2. Now Peter fell in love all with
A nice young girl,
The first three letters of her name
Were Lu-ci-ana Pearl.
CHORUS

3. Just as they were about to wed
Her father did say no,
And consequently she was sent
Beyond the O-hi-o.
CHORUS

4. When Peter heard his love was lost,
He knew not what to say;
He'd half a mind to jump into
The Susquehan-i-a.
CHORUS

5. But Peter went away out West
For furs and other skins,
But he got caught an scalp-i-ed
By a bloody In-ji-an.
CHORUS

6. When Lucianna heard the news
She straightway went to bed,
And never did get up again
Until she di-i-ed.
CHORUS

7. You fathers all a warning take,
Each one as has a girl,
And think upon poor Peter Gray
And Lu-ci-anna Pearl.
CHORUS

POOR ELLEN SMITH

Ukulele tuning: gCEA

TRADITIONAL

1.Poor El - len Smith, how she was found, shot through the heart ly - ing cold on the ground. Her clothes were all scat - tered and thrown on the ground and blood marks the spot where poor El - len was found.

POOR ELLEN SMITH

2. They picked up her body and carried it away,
And now she is sleeping in some lonesome old grave.
They picked up their rifles and hunted me down
And found me a-loafin' in Mount Airy Town.

3. I brushed back my tears when the people all said
It was Peter de Graff who shot Ellen Smith dead.
The judge he will hang me, he will if he can,
God knows if they hang me I'm an innocent man.

4. I've been in this prison for twenty long years,
Each night I see Ellen through my bitter tears.
The warden just told me that soon I'll be free
To go to her grave 'neath that old willow tree.

5. I got me a letter and I read it today,
Poor Ellen's flowers have all faded away.
Some day I'll go home and when I do go,
On poor Ellen's grave pretty flowers I'll sow.

6. My days in this prison are ending at last,
But I'll never be free from the sins of my past.
Poor Ellen Smith, how she was found,
Shot through her heart lying cold on the ground.

Although this song indicates that the alleged muderer, Peter de Graff, was imprisoned and released, in reality he was convicted and executed despite his claim of innocence. Many versions of this song exist with interchanged lyrics and melodies. Surprisingly, one version sets the song's melody to the well-known hymn *How Firm A Foundation*.

SAM HALL

Ukulele tuning: gCEA

TRADITIONAL

2. Oh, I killed a man they said, so they said,
Yes, I killed a man they said, so they said,
Yes, I killed a man they said,
And I filled him full of lead,
And I left him there for dead,
Blast your eyes.

SAM HALL

3. To the gallows I must go, I must go,
To the gallows I must go, I must go,
To the gallows I must go
With my friends all down below
Yelling, "Sam, I told you so!'
 Blast their eyes!

4. Oh, the preacher he did come, he did come,
Oh, the preacher he did come, he did come,
Oh, the preacher he did come,
And he looked so awful glum
As he talked of Kingdom Come,
Blast his eyes.

5. Oh, the sheriff he came too, he came too,
Yes, the sheriff he came too, he came too,
Oh, the sheriff he came too
With his little boys in blue,
And I hope they sizzle too,
Blast their eyes.

6. I saw Nellie in the crowd, in the crowd,
I saw Nellie in the crowd, in the crowd,
I saw Nellie in the crowd
And I shouted right out loud,
Yelling, "Nellie, Ain't you proud?"
Blast your eyes.

7. Let this be my parting knell, parting knell,
Let this be my parting knell, parting knell,
Let this be my parting knell:
I will see you all in Hell,
And I hope you sizzle well,
Blast your eyes.

SPRINGFIELD MOUNTAIN

SPRINGFIELD MOUNTAIN

2. This lovely youth one day did go
Down to the meadow for to mow.
CHORUS

3. He had not mowed quite round the field
When an ugly serpent bit on his heel.
CHORUS

4. They took him home to Molly dear
Which made him feel so very queer.
CHORUS

5. Now Molly had two ruby lips
With which the poison she did sip.
CHORUS

6. But Molly had a rotten tooth
And so the poison killed them both.
CHORUS

ST. JAMES INFIRMARY BLUES

Ukulele tuning: gCEA

TRADITIONAL

ST. JAMES INFIRMARY BLUES

I went down to old Joe's barroom
On the corner by the square,
The drinks were served as usual,1
And the usual crowd was there.

On my left stood Joe McGinty,
His eyes were bloodshot red,
He turned to the crowd around him,
And these were the words that he said:

"I went down to St. Jame's Infirmary
To see my Baby there,
She was stretched out on a long white table,
So sweet, so cold, so fair."

Let her go, let her go, God bless her,
Wherever she may be,
You can search this wide world over,
And never find another girl as sweet as she.

There are six men going to the graveyard,
Six in an old-time hack,
Six men going to the graveyard,
But only five are coming back.

When I die, please be sure to bury me
In my high-top Stetson hat,
Put a twenty-dollar gold piece on my watch chain,
So the gang'll know I died standing pat.

I want six crap shooters for my pall bearers,
A chorus girl to sing me a song,
Put a jazz band on my hearse wagon
To raise some hell as we roll along.

And now that you've heard my story,
Let's all have another shot of booze,
And if anyone should happen to ask you,
Well, I've got those gambler's blues.

STREETS OF LAREDO

Ukulele tuning: gCEA

TRADITIONAL

STREETS OF LAREDO

2. "I see by your outfit that you are a cowboy,"
These words I did say as I boldly stepped by.
"Come sit down beside me and hear my sad story,
I'm shot in the breast and I know I must die.

3. "It was once in the saddle I used to go dashing,
Once in the saddle I used to go gay,
First to the card house and then down to Rosie's,
I'm shot in the breast and I'm dying today.

4. "Get six jolly cowboys to carry my coffin,
Get six pretty maidens to carry my pall,
Put bunches of roses all over my coffin,
Roses to deaden the clods as they fall.

5. "Oh, beat the drum slowly and play the fife lowly,
Play the dead march as you carry me along.
Take me to the green valley and lay the sod o'er me,
For I'm a young cowboy and I know I've done wrong."

OVER there through the shadows
I see a camp fire gleam
And there's a pony grazin'
Beside a peaceful stream.
Is that bacon I smell fryin'?
Yep! and a pot o' coffee too.
And there's a cowboy spreadin' his blanket–
Don't yuh wish you was him? I do!

Carson J. Robison

TAM PEARSE

Ukulele tuning: gCEA

TRADITIONAL

♩=180

1.Tam Pearse, Tam Pearse lend me your grey mare,

all a - long, down a - long, out a - long lea, for

us wants to go___ to Wid - e-combe Fair with Bill

Brew - er, Jan Stew - er, Pet - er Gur - ney, Pet - er, Dav - y, Dan -'l

TAM PEARSE

Wid - don, Har - ry Hawke, old Un - cle Tom Cob - ley and

all, _____ old Un - cle Tom Cob - ley and all. _____

2. And when shall I see again my old grey mare,
All along, down along, out along lea?
By Friday noon or Saturday soon
With Bill Brewer, Jan Stewer, etc.

3. Friday came and Saturday soon,
All along, down along, out along lea,
But Tam Pearse n'er did see his old mare come home
With Bill Brewer, Jan Stewer, etc.

4. Tam he went to the top of the hill,
All along, down along, out along lea,
And he sees his old grey mare a-making her will
With Bill Brewer, Jan Stewer, etc.

5. When the wind blows cold on the moor of a night,
All along, down along, out along lea,
Tam Pearse's grey mare appears ghastly white,
With Bll Brewer, Jan Stewer, etc.

THREE RAVENS

Ukulele tuning: gCEA

TRADITIONAL

2. Then one of them said to his mate,
Downe a downe a downe,
Then one of them said to his mate,
"Where shall we our breakfast take?"
Downe a downe a derrie derrie downe.

THREE RAVENS

3. Down in yonder green field
   Downe a downe a downe
Down in yonder green field
There lies a knight beneath his shield,
   Downe a downe a derrie derrie downe.

4. His hounds they lie down at his feet,
So well they can their master keep.

5. His hawks they fly so eagerly,
There's no foul dare him come nigh.

6. Down there comes a fallow doe,
As great with young as she might go.

7. She lifted up his bloody head,
And kissed his wounds that were so red.

8. She got him up upon her back,
And carried him to earthen lak.*

9.She buried him before the prime,
She was dead herself ere even time.

10 God send every gentleman,
Such hawks, such hounds, and such a leman.*

*lak=lake
*leman = sweetheart

Reference to a "fallow doe" is thought to be a metaphor for a pregnant lover.

TIT-WILLOW

ARTHUR SULLIVAN

Ukulele tuning: gCEA

W.S. GILBERT

"Tit Willow" is a selection from the comic opera "The Mikado" by the celebrated team of Gilbert and Sullivan. Many of their other popular songs are available for the ukulele from the catalog of Centerstream Music.

TIT-WILLOW

2. He slapped at his chest, as he sat on that bough,
   Singing "Willow, tit-willow, tit-willow!"
   And a cold perspiration bespangled his brow,
   Oh, Willow, tit-willow, tit-willow!
   He sobbed and he sighed, and a gurgle he gave,
   Then he plunged himself into the billowy wave,
   And an echo arose from the suicide's grave,
   "Oh, Willow, tit-willow, tit-willow!"

3. Now I feel just as sure as I'm sure that my name
   Isn't Willow, tit-willow, tit-willow,
   That 'twas blighted affection that made him exclaim,
   "Oh, Willow, tit-willow, tit-willow!"
   And if you remain callous and obdurate, I
   Shall perish as he did, and you will know why,
   Though I probably shall not exclaim as I die,
   "Oh, Willow, tit-willow, tit-willow!"

TOM DOOLEY

Ukulele tuning: gCEA

TRADITIONAL

TOM DOOLEY

2. This time tomorrow, reckon where I'll be,
In some lonesome valley, hanging from a white oak tree.
CHORUS

3. This time tomorrow, reckon where I'll be,
If it hadn't been for Grayson I'd be in Tennessee.
CHORUS

Tom Dula, a North Carolinian, was a real-life person, accused of killing his girl friend, Laura Foster. Suspected of the murder, Dula tried to outrun the law and took refuge in Tennessee working on the farm of Col. James Grayson who subsequently helped capture Dula and return him to North Carolina. Dula was tried, convicted, and sentenced to death by hanging. This folk ballad, written after Dula's death in 1868, changed his name to Dooley, which is how the name was pronounced in Appalachian dialect.

The version of "Tom Dooley" recorded by the popular folk-pop group The Kingston Trio hit the charts in October of 1958 and climbed to the Number One position the next month. Over three million copies were sold as a single.

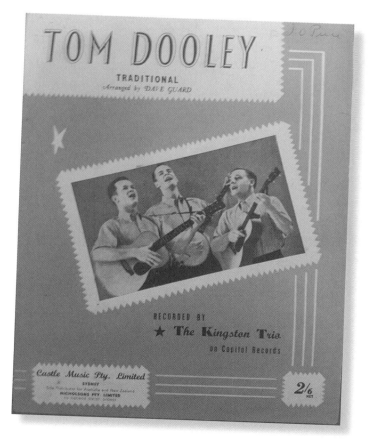

UNFORTUNATE MISS BAILEY

Ukulele tuning: gCEA

TRADITIONAL

With an easy swing.

1.A cap - tain bold from Hal - i-fax who dwelt in coun - try quar - ters, se -

duced a maid who hanged her - self one Mon - day in her gar - ters. His

wick - ed con - science smit - ed him he lost his stom - ach dail - y, he

took to drink - ing rat - a - fia and thought up - on Miss Bail - ey.

UNFORTUNATE MISS BAILEY

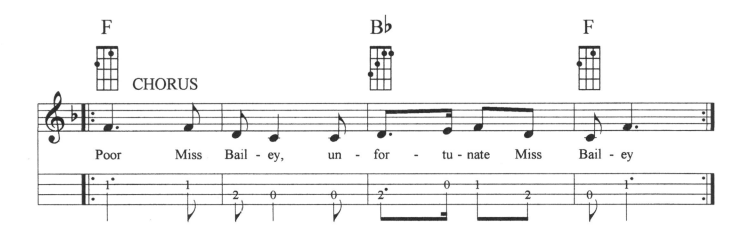

CHORUS

Poor Miss Bail - ey, un - for - tu - nate Miss Bail - ey

2. One night betimes he went to bed, for he had caught a fever,
Said he, "I am a handsome man and I'm a gay deceiver."
His candle just at twelve o'clock began to burn quite paley,
A ghost stepped up to his bedside and said, "Behold Miss Bailey!"
CHORUS

3. "Avaunt, Miss Bailey," then he cried, "you can't affright me, really."
"Dear Captain Smith," the ghost replied, "you've used me ungenteely.
The coroner's quest was hard with me because I've acted frailly,
And Parson Briggs won't bury me, though I'm a dead Miss Bailey."
CHORUS

4. "Miss Bailey, then, since you and I accounts must now we close,
I've got a five-pound note in my regimental small-clothes.
'Twill bribe the sexton for your grave." The ghost then vanished gaily,
Crying, "Bless you, wicked Captain Smith, remember poor Miss Bailey."
CHORUS

WRECK OF THE OLD NINETY-SEVEN

Ukulele tuning: gCEA

TRADITIONAL

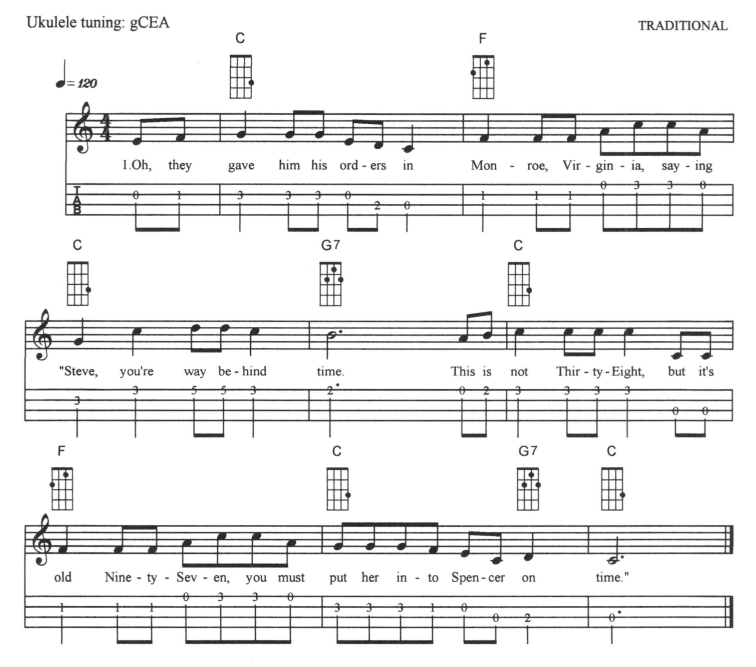

2. Well, they gave him his orders at Monroe, Virginia,
Said, "Steve, you're way behind time,
This is not 38, this is ol' 97
Put her into Spencer on time."

3. Then Steve turned around to his black, greasy fireman,
Saying, "Shovel on a little more coal,
And when we cross that White Oak Mountain,
Watch ol' 97 roll."

4. It's a mighty rough road from Lynchburg to Danville
For the line has a three-mile grade.
It was on that grade that he lost his airbrakes,
And you see what a jump that he made.

5. He was going down the grade making 90 miles an hour
When the whistle broke into a scream;
He was found in the wreck with his hand on the throttle,
Scalded to death by the steam.

6. Then a telegram came from the Washington station,
And this is how that telegam read:
Oh, that brave engineer that run ol' 97
Is lying now in Danville dead.

7. So come all you ladies, you'd better take warning
From this time on and learn,
Never speak hard words to your true-loving husband,
He may leave you and never return.

More Great Books from Dick Sheridan...